The Importance of Spiritual Discernment

Bisi Oladipupo

Springs of life publishing

Copyright © 2022 by Bisi Oladipupo

Springs of life publishing

ISBN: 978-1-915269-20-1 (ePub e-book)

ISBN: 978-1-915269-19-5 (paperback)

All Rights Reserved.

No part of this book may be used or reproduced by any means, graphic, electronic, or mechanical, including photocopying, recording, taping, or by any information storage retrieval system without the written permission of the publisher except in the case of brief quotations embodied in critical articles and reviews.

Unless otherwise indicated, scripture quotations are taken from the King James Version.

Scripture quotations from The Authorized (King James) Version. Rights in the Authorized Version in the United Kingdom are vested in the Crown. Reproduced by permission of the Crown's patentee, Cambridge University Press.

Scripture taken from the New King James Version®. Copyright © 1982 by Thomas Nelson. Used by permission. All rights reserved.

Contents

Dedication	V
Foreword	VI
1. Why Discernment?	1
2. The Life of Our Lord Jesus Christ and Spiritual Discernment	3
3. Spiritual Discernment in the life of Paul	13
4. Discerning Our True Spiritual Condition	15
5. Hindrances to lack of discernment	18
6. Other Things We Need to Discern	29
7. Scriptures about Discernment	36
8. How to Sharpen Our Discernment	39
9. Cost of Lack of Discernment	44
10. Good News	46
11. Conclusion	48
Salvation Prayer	49
About The Author	50

Also By Bisi

To Jesus Christ my Lord and saviour; to Him alone that laid down His life that l might have life eternal. To Him that lead captivity captive and gave gifts unto men (Ephesians 4; 8). One of those gifts is writing!.

Bisi Oladipupo

Foreword

So, what is discernment?

Discernment, in my own words, is the ability to know exactly what is going on behind a person's words, actions, or the root cause of a situation.

Therefore, spiritual discernment is basically the same: the ability to discern what is going on spiritually. So, for example, a person's words may be saying one thing, while spiritual discernment will help identify the root cause of the problem.

After formulating my definition of discernment, I checked out the meaning online. One of the definitions I discovered is that discernment is "the quality of being able to grasp and comprehend what is obscure" (Merriam-Webster Dictionary).

So, why is spiritual discernment so necessary?

THE IMPORTANCE OF SPIRITUAL DISCERN...

The Holy Spirit has been given to us, and one of His functions is to guide us into "all truth". If we do not walk in discernment, we can easily end up in many unwanted situations. For instance, when we relate to others, we might think a person is our best friend, only down the line to find out that they actually did not like us at all.

Spiritual discernment is so essential when counselling others and in our everyday life. Sometimes, people will only tell you what they want you to know, but spiritual discernment will expose the truth of the situation.

When we look at the life of Jesus Christ, our Lord was never caught unawares. He knew what was happening behind the scenes, even to the minute of a person's thoughts.

This book will look at examples from our Lord Jesus Christ's life and other parts of Scripture to examine the importance of discernment and how we can sharpen it.

Chapter 1

Why Discernment?

Discernment is necessary in every area of our lives and when relating to others. As mentioned previously, without discernment, we can fall prey to unpleasant situations and unnecessary hard times. Have you ever looked back at a problem and said, "I sensed that was the case, but why did I not listen to that check in my spirit"?

We must remember that the Holy Spirit has been sent to guide us into all truth (John 16:13). Therefore, we must learn how to cooperate and yield to His leading.

We will save ourselves from difficult relationships and complex situations. Also, we won't be deceived by others and will find it easier to minister to people when we walk in discernment. Finally, we will not end up in the wrong places when we walk in discernment.

Our God is merciful and will always rescue us from situations we have found ourselves due to lack of discernment. First, however, we need to learn and mature in this area.

Jesus Christ, our Lord, walked in spiritual discernment, and we will look at examples from Scripture.

Chapter 2

The Life of Our Lord Jesus Christ and Spiritual Discernment

Jesus Knew When Virtue Left Him

Jesus Christ, our Lord, walked in so much power that He knew when power left Him. So, as our Lord Jesus Christ walked as a man during His anointed earthly ministry, He had to sense things and use discernment like we do.

Jesus knew that virtue had left Him, but He did not know what happened at that point. This account can be found when the woman with the issue of blood touched Jesus Christ our Lord:

*"And a woman having an issue of blood twelve years, which had spent all her living upon physicians, neither could be healed of any, Came behind him, and touched the border of his garment: and immediately her issue of blood stanched. And Jesus said, Who touched me? When all denied, Peter and they that were with him said, Master, the multitude throng thee and press thee, and sayest thou, Who touched me? And Jesus said, **Somebody hath touched me: for I perceive that virtue is gone out of me**"* (Luke 8:43-46).

It is only after Jesus asked the question that the woman admitted and said what happened:

"And when the woman saw that she was not hid, she came trembling, and falling down before him, she declared unto him before all the people for what cause she had touched him, and how she was healed immediately" (Luke 8:47).

Isn't this good to know that our Lord Jesus Christ knew when power left Him?

If we are to be effective Christians, we need to know when power leaves us and when we need a refill. If

THE IMPORTANCE OF SPIRITUAL DISCERN...

we are not sensitive to this, it will eventually catch up on us.

If power left you, you simply need a refill by returning to God's presence. This probably explains why some people end up feeling drained. They have been giving out and not knowing that virtue has left them, and they need to be filled back up.

This is one reason we need to spend time in God's presence and His Word.

I recently watched an online conference where the man of God called out those who wanted him to lay hands on them. A crowd came out. He then started laying hands on them and suddenly he stopped, and said, *"If l continue this, l will be drained"*. So, he instructed those who came forward to join hands together, and he prayed for them jointly.

This man of God had discernment and knew he could not afford to be drained.

Jesus Christ Our Lord Discerned the Reason Behind a Physical Infirmity

When we read Scripture, we learn that Jesus healed sickness and disease in different ways. One thing that determined how the Lord administered healing was the ability to discern the root cause of the illness. Hence, we need the help of the Holy Spirit to be able to discern the root cause of an illness.

Let us see a few examples of how Jesus Christ our Lord healed people:

*"And he was teaching in one of the synagogues on the sabbath. And, behold, there was a woman **which had a spirit of infirmity eighteen years, and was bowed together,** and could in no wise lift up herself. And when Jesus saw her, he called her to him, and said unto her, Woman, **thou art loosed from thine infirmity**. And he laid his hands on her: and immediately she was made straight, and glorified God"* (Luke 13:10-13).

From this account, we can see this woman was bowed down because she had a spirit of infirmity.

*"And again, departing from the coasts of Tyre and Sidon, he came unto the sea of Galilee, through the midst of the coasts of Decapolis. And they bring unto him one that was deaf, and had an impediment in his speech; and they beseech him to put his hand upon him. And he took him aside from the multitude, and put his fingers into his ears, and he spit, and touched his tongue; And looking up to heaven, he sighed, and saith unto him, Ephphatha, that is, Be opened. And straightway his ears were opened, **and***

the string of his tongue was loosed, and he spake plain" (Mark 7:31-35).

If you look at the last phrase, it says, "the string of his tongue was loosed". This was not a natural string. In the spirit, this man's tongue must have been tied and now loosed after Jesus spoke to him.

Jesus Discerned the Thoughts of People

During the earthly ministry of Jesus Christ our Lord, He discerned people's thoughts without them saying anything.

In this situation, the scribes thought within themselves if Jesus Christ would heal this person. Jesus Christ knew their thoughts and addressed them:

"*And he entered into a ship, and passed over, and came into his own city. And, behold, they brought to him a man sick of the palsy, lying on a bed: and Jesus seeing their faith said unto the sick of the palsy; Son, be of good cheer; thy sins be forgiven thee.* ***And, behold, certain of the scribes said within themselves, This man blasphemeth. And Jesus knowing their thoughts said, Wherefore think ye evil in your hearts?*** *For whether is easier, to say, Thy sins be forgiven thee; or to say, Arise, and walk*"? (Matthew 9:1-5).

In this account, the disciples were reasoning who would be the greatest amongst them. Although this account is quite interesting, the Bible says there was a reasoning amongst them. In other words, it was just in their thinking, and Jesus Christ addressed it:

"***Then there arose a reasoning among them***, *which of them should be greatest. And **Jesus, perceiving the thought of their heart**, took a child, and set him by him, And said unto them, Whosoever shall receive this child in my name receiveth me: and whosoever shall receive me receiveth him that sent me: for he that is least among you all, the same shall be great*" (Luke 9:46-48).

After the miracle of five loaves and two fishes, the people wanted to take Jesus by force and make Him king. Jesus Christ perceived their intent, and He avoided it:

"*Then those men, when they had seen the miracle that Jesus did, said, This is of a truth that prophet that should come into the world. **When Jesus therefore perceived that they would come and take him by force, to make him a king**, he departed again into a mountain himself alone*" (John 6:14-15).

We can learn from our Lord Jesus Christ and become more sensitive to our environments.

Jesus Christ Discerned the Motives of People

Have you ever been caught unawares by someone in your sphere of influence? Suddenly, you saw another side of them you never expected? Unfortunately, many of us have experienced this when relating to others.

Do you know that Jesus Christ our Lord was never caught unawares?

We know Judas Iscariot betrayed Jesus Christ our Lord, but did you know it did not catch our Lord unawares?

Also, in Scripture, we see some disciples turned back from following the Lord when they did not understand what He said. So, this too did not take our Lord by surprise:

"He that eateth my flesh, and drinketh my blood, dwelleth in me, and I in him. As the living Father hath sent me, and I live by the Father: so he that eateth me, even he shall live by me. This is that bread which came down from heaven: not as your fathers did eat manna, and are dead: he that eateth of this bread shall live for ever. These things said he in the synagogue, as he taught in Capernaum. Many therefore of his disciples, when they had heard this,

said, This is an hard saying; who can hear it? ***When Jesus knew in himself that his disciples murmured at it, he said unto them, Doth this offend you?*** *What and if ye shall see the Son of man ascend up where he was before? It is the spirit that quickeneth; the flesh profiteth nothing: the words that I speak unto you, they are spirit, and they are life. But there are some of you that believe not.* ***For Jesus knew from the beginning who they were that believed not, and who should betray him.*** *And he said, Therefore said I unto you, that no man can come unto me, except it were given unto him of my Father.* ***From that time many of his disciples went back, and walked no more with him***" (John 6:56-66).

From this scripture, we can see that Jesus Christ our Lord knew when the disciples murmured, those that believed not, and who should betray Him.

When the Pharisees tried to catch Jesus in His talk, our Lord Jesus Christ perceived their wickedness:

"*Then went the Pharisees, and took counsel how they might entangle him in his talk. And they sent out unto him their disciples with the Herodians, saying, Master, we know that thou art true, and teachest the way of God in truth, neither carest thou for any man: for thou regardest not the person of men. Tell us therefore, What thinkest thou? Is it lawful to give tribute unto Caesar, or not?*

But Jesus perceived their wickedness, and said, Why tempt ye me, ye hypocrites"? (Matthew 22:15-18).

Jesus Knew the Spiritual Condition of His Loved Ones

Our Lord Jesus Christ prayed for His own (John 17:9), and our Lord was well aware of the enemy's plans for Simon Peter even before it happened:

"*And the Lord said, Simon, Simon, behold, Satan hath desired to have you, that he may sift you as wheat:* ***But I have prayed for thee****, that thy faith fail not: and when thou art converted, strengthen thy brethren*" (Luke 22:31-32).

Our Lord Jesus Christ cared for His own and prayed for them.

When they told Jesus Christ our Lord that Lazarus was sick, He knew when Lazarus had died before He got there. Nobody told Him. The only message that was relayed to our saviour was that Lazarus was sick:

"*Now a certain man was sick, named Lazarus, of Bethany, the town of Mary and her sister Martha. (It was that Mary which anointed the Lord with ointment, and wiped his feet with her hair, whose brother Lazarus was sick.)* ***Therefore his sisters sent unto him, saying, Lord, behold, he whom thou lovest is sick*** (John 11:1-3).

These things said he: and after that he saith unto them, Our friend Lazarus sleepeth; but I go, that I may awake him out of sleep. Then said his disciples, Lord, if he sleep, he shall do well. Howbeit Jesus spake of his death: but they thought that he had spoken of taking of rest in sleep. **Then said Jesus unto them plainly, Lazarus is dead** (John 11:11-13).

We can see that the sisters' message to Jesus Christ our Lord stated: "Lazarus is sick!" This must have been the situation then. We must remember that they had no cars in those days, so journeys took longer. Jesus Christ knew Lazarus was dead.

We can see that our Lord Jesus Christ had great sensitivity and discernment during His earthly ministry.

Chapter 3

Spiritual Discernment in the life of Paul

Paul was being taken to Italy alongside other prisoners. During the trip, Paul perceived that the ship and the lives of those on board the vessel were in danger. However, this could not have been obvious on the outside, as the centurion did not believe Paul:

*"Now when much time was spent, and when sailing was now dangerous, because the fast was now already past, Paul admonished them, And said unto them, **Sirs, I perceive that this voyage will be with hurt and much damage, not only of the lading and ship, but also***

of our lives. Nevertheless the centurion believed the master and the owner of the ship, more than those things which were spoken by Paul" (Acts 27:9-11).

So, we can see that Paul's words were not believed until they got into trouble. The rest of the account can be found in Acts 27:11-44. All this could have been avoided if the centurion had listened to Paul.

This is what Paul had to say amid the difficulty:

"But after long abstinence Paul stood forth in the midst of them, and said, Sirs, ye should have hearkened unto me, and not have loosed from Crete, and to have gained this harm and loss" (Acts 27:21).

Paul's discernment would have saved all those that sailed with him from the difficult time they went through had they listened to Paul.

# Chapter 4

Discerning Our True Spiritual Condition

Yes, we now know the Lord and are born again by the Spirit of God and while we rejoice in that, what is our relational position with God?

We all need to walk with the Lord as closely as we know how.

One church in the Book of Revelation did not know they were lukewarm until they were told. So, is it possible to be lukewarm and not be aware? From this account, yes, it is possible:

*"I know thy works, that thou art neither cold nor hot: I would thou wert cold or hot. So then because thou art lukewarm, and neither cold nor hot, I will spue thee out of my mouth. **Because thou sayest, I am rich, and increased with goods, and have need of nothing; and knowest not that thou art wretched, and miserable, and poor, and blind, and naked:***" (Revelation 3:15-17).

This church had riches and thought they needed nothing, yet they did not know they were wretched, miserable, poor, blind, and naked. That was their true spiritual condition.

Is the Lord trying to call you into a deeper walk with Him? Has the Lord placed people around you that you desire the level of their closeness with the Lord? Could the Lord be waiting for you to respond?

We are all called to know the Lord:

"And this is life eternal, that they might know thee the only true God, and Jesus Christ, whom thou hast sent" (John 17:3).

Part of our new covenant is to know and walk with God:

"For this is the covenant that I will make with the house of Israel after those days, saith the Lord; I will put my laws into their mind, and write them in their hearts: and I will

be to them a God, and they shall be to me a people: And they shall not teach every man his neighbour, and every man his brother, saying, Know the Lord: for all shall know me, from the least to the greatest. For I will be merciful to their unrighteousness, and their sins and their iniquities will I remember no more. In that he saith, A new covenant, he hath made the first old. Now that which decayeth and waxeth old is ready to vanish away" (Hebrews 8:10-13).

Chapter 5

Hindrances to lack of discernment

There are many factors that contribute to the lack of discernment. Let us have a look at some of them.

Immaturity

Immaturity in both the natural and spiritual is the leading cause of lack of discernment. It's like a parent dissuading their daughter from marrying a certain person because the parents are more mature and can already discern that their daughter is heading for danger.

THE IMPORTANCE OF SPIRITUAL DISCERN...

There could be many reasons a parent does not want their son or daughter to marry an individual, and while sometimes these reasons are not always justified, it is good to listen to parents.

Most parents have the best interest of their children at heart and have enough maturity to foresee dangers that their children are too young to perceive.

I remembered a few years ago, l was watching a live stream ministration of a church service. The minister has a powerful prophetic ministry. He then called out a lady and told her she was in a mess in her marriage because she did not listen to her parents. What surprised me was that her parents were not even Christians, and neither was she before she was called out. This shows parents have a level of discernment and maturity that children do not have, simply because they lack experience. In this case, the Lord said He would have mercy on her, and things would work out.

Have you ever looked back and said, "My parents told me this several years ago; l wish l had listened"? That is an excellent example of immaturity.

The same applies spiritually, which is why we need more mature believers around us. Most people make decisions based on their maturity and level of discernment at that time. But unfortunately, sometimes, it takes incidents that will trigger a wake-up call that something is not right.

Not Asking for Counsel

There is a reason why we are told to acknowledge the Lord in all our ways, and He will direct our paths (Proverbs 3:6). There are so many things we don't know; we really need to commit all our ways unto the Lord.

A classic example of this is can be found in the Book of Joshua:

"And it came to pass, when all the kings which were on this side Jordan, in the hills, and in the valleys, and in all the coasts of the great sea over against Lebanon, the Hittite, and the Amorite, the Canaanite, the Perizzite, the Hivite, and the Jebusite, heard thereof; That they gathered themselves together, to fight with Joshua and with Israel, with one accord. And when the inhabitants of Gibeon heard what Joshua had done unto Jericho and to Ai, They did work wilily, and went and made as if they had been ambassadors, and took old sacks upon their asses, and wine bottles, old, and rent, and bound up; And old shoes and clouted upon their feet, and old garments upon them; and all the bread of their provision was dry and mouldy. And they went to Joshua unto the camp at Gilgal, and said unto him, and to the men of Israel, We be come from a far

THE IMPORTANCE OF SPIRITUAL DISCERN...

country: now therefore make ye a league with us. And the men of Israel said unto the Hivites, Peradventure ye dwell among us; and how shall we make a league with you?" (Joshua 9:1-7).

These men came to Joshua and pretended as if they had been on a long journey. The evidence they produced included:

- Old sacks
- Old wine bottles
- Old shoes
- Old garments
- Mouldy and dry bread

This is the evidence they presented to Joshua and the men of Israel that they came from a far country.

The truth is that without spiritual discernment and allowing the Lord to direct, anyone would fall prey to this.

This is one reason why the benefits of a job might look good with an excellent salary, and the Holy Spirit might say, "Don't take that job". We really need to lean on the Lord in all our decisions.

Joshua fell prey to this and made a covenant with these people because they succeeded in deceiving them with natural things.

The entire account can be found in Joshua 9:1-27.

Here, we can see the men speaking to Joshua and the men of Israel:

"This our bread we took hot for our provision out of our houses on the day we came forth to go unto you; but now, behold, it is dry, and it is mouldy: And these bottles of wine, which we filled, were new; and, behold, they be rent: and these our garments and our shoes are become old by reason of the very long journey. **And the men took of their victuals, and asked not counsel at the mouth of the Lord.** *And Joshua made peace with them, and made a league with them, to let them live: and the princes of the congregation sware unto them"* (Joshua 9:12-15).

"And it came to pass at the end of three days after *they had made a league with them, that they heard that they were their neighbours, and that they dwelt among them. And the children of Israel journeyed, and came unto their cities on the third day. Now their cities were Gibeon, and Chephirah, and Beeroth, and Kirjathjearim. And the children of Israel smote them not, because the princes of the congregation had sworn unto them by the Lord God of Israel. And all the congregation murmured against the princes"* (Josuha 9:16-18).

THE IMPORTANCE OF SPIRITUAL DISCERN...

Before we start throwing stones at these men, how many of us have gotten involved in something appealing, only after a short while, to discover that we had made a mistake?

Thank God we can learn from our mistakes and move unto wiser and better decisions by engaging the Lord and the Holy Spirit in all we do.

Natural Reasoning

This is another factor that can affect our discernment when we override things that are supposed to catch our attention with natural reasoning. This is what happened to Eve in the garden of Eden.

Examining the conversation between the serpent and Eve, the serpent had already started the conversation by saying what God did not say. The serpent said, *"You shall not eat of every tree of the garden"*. If you look at the verse, it was the woman who corrected the serpent by revealing the only tree God said they must not eat.

Should that not have caught her attention? Can l really trust what is being said here, considering l just gave the correct version?

And before we start throwing stones, many of us have experienced where something triggered a cause to be cautious, but we still went ahead.

"Now the serpent was more cunning than any beast of the field which the Lord God had made. And he said to the woman, "Has God indeed said, 'You shall not eat of every tree of the garden'?" And the woman said to the serpent, "We may eat the fruit of the trees of the garden; but of the fruit of the tree which is in the midst of the garden, God has said, 'You shall not eat it, nor shall you touch it, lest you die.' " Then the serpent said to the woman, "You will not surely die. For God knows that in the day you eat of it your eyes will be opened, and you will be like God, knowing good and evil." So when the woman saw that the tree was good for food, that it was ⁰pleasant to the eyes, and a tree desirable to make one wise, she took of its fruit and ate. She also gave to her husband with her, and he ate. Then the eyes of both of them were opened, and they knew that they were naked; and they sewed fig leaves together and made themselves ⁰coverings" (Genesis 3:1-7; NKJV).

Eve's natural reasoning overrides the warning she had from the serpent initially, not giving her an accurate account of what God said.

Have you ever met someone and the person said something, or you got an impression that things are not all they seem to be? You still go ahead only to find that the initial signs were true.

Not Obeying the Word of God

We must realise that God and His Word are one. Therefore, when the Holy Spirit tells us something, we must know He is taking from Jesus Christ and showing it unto us:

"For he shall not speak of himself; but whatsoever he shall hear, that shall he speak (John 16:14).

"For there are three that bear record in heaven, the Father, the Word, and the Holy Ghost: and these three are one" (1 John 5:7).

Therefore, we hinder our discernment when the Holy Spirit tells us something or God's Word clearly states or reveals something, and we violate it.

Under the chapter of "spiritual discernment in the life of Paul", we found the account where those he was with in the ship did not listen to what he said, which caused them problems that could have been avoided (Acts 27).

We must always obey the Word of God and whatever the Holy Spirit tells us in any situation.

Lack of Spiritual Growth

Growing up spiritually is for our own good in so many ways. However, in the natural, there are certain things you will not be able to discuss with a child as they would not have the capacity to understand what you are saying.

The same applies spiritually, and this also relates to our discernment.

Have you ever been part of something and thought everything was going great? Then, after a couple of years, you suddenly have the ability to discern that something is not quite right.

Therefore, we need to listen to those that have gone ahead of us, as due to growth, they will have the capacity to pick up things we may not be able to discern at that time in our lives.

"As newborn babes, desire the sincere milk of the word, that ye may grow thereby" (1 Peter 2:2).

"Of whom we have many things to say, and hard to be uttered, seeing ye are dull of hearing. For when for the time ye ought to be teachers, ye have need that one teach you again which be the first principles of the oracles of God; and are become such as have need of milk, and not of strong meat. For every one that useth milk is unskilful

in the word of righteousness: for he is a babe. But strong meat belongeth to them that are of full age, even those who by reason of use have their senses exercised to discern both good and evil" (Hebrews 5:11-14).

We can see from the above scriptures that it takes spiritual growth to be able to discern both good and evil.

Wrong Mindsets

When our thinking is wrong, we will not be open to certain things, which can hinder us from discerning what is actually happening.

Having a wrong mindset or perspective about a subject matter will hinder discernment. For example, have you ever told someone before: "There is no point in telling them; they simply will not understand"? That is an example of a wrong mindset.

When David sent some of his servants to go and comfort Hanun because of his father's death, the people of Ammon had a wrong perspective about the matter.

"And the princes of the people of Ammon said to Hanun their lord, "Do you think that David really honors your father because he has sent comforters to you? Has David not rather sent his servants to you to search the city, to

spy it out, and to overthrow it?" Therefore Hanun took David's servants, shaved off half of their beards, cut off their garments in the middle, at their buttocks, and sent them away" (2 Samuel 10:3-4; NKJV).

Their wrong mindset caused them not to discern the sincerity of David's intention to comfort Hanun.

This can happen to anyone of us. Has anyone misunderstood your sincere motives? A wrong mindset can result in people lacking real discernment about a matter.

Unbelief

Unbelief can also hinder true discernment. Again, we can see an example of this in Scripture:

"O Jerusalem, Jerusalem, the one who kills the prophets and stones those who are sent to her! How often I wanted to gather your children together, as a hen gathers her chicks under her wings, but you were not willing! See! Your house is left to you desolate; for I say to you, you shall see Me no more till you say, 'Blessed is He who comes in the name of the Lord!'" (Matthew 23:37-39; NJKV).

We can see from this scripture that they missed out because they did not receive the prophets and those sent to them.

Chapter 6

Other Things We Need to Discern

So, what other things do we need to discern? Perhaps we should put it another way: what things are wise to discern?

As Christians, we are now in the Spirit (Romans 8:9) and told to walk in the Spirit (Galatians 5:25). Therefore, we need to start discerning things after the Spirit.

The Lord's Body

We are instructed to discern the Lord's body. There are two applications to this.

The first application is to discern the price the Lord has paid for us and Him bearing our sins, sicknesses, and diseases:

"Who his own self bare our sins in his own body on the tree, that we, being dead to sins, should live unto righteousness: by whose stripes ye were healed" (1 Peter 2:24).

The above scripture shows us what Jesus Christ did for us in His body.

In the ordinance of breaking bread normally called "the Lord's supper" (1 Cor. 11: 20), we are told the consequences of not discerning the Lord's body:

*"Wherefore whosoever shall eat this bread, and drink this cup of the Lord, unworthily, shall be guilty of the body and blood of the Lord. But let a man examine himself, and so let him eat of that bread, and drink of that cup. For he that eateth and drinketh unworthily, eateth and drinketh damnation to himself, **not discerning the Lord's body**. For this cause many are weak and sickly among you, and many sleep. For if we would judge ourselves, we should not be judged"* (1 Corinthians 11:27-31).

We can find the context of the above scripture in the preceding verses (1 Corinthians 11:18-22). Here, Paul spoke about divisions, heresies, drunkenness, etc. Therefore, we must contextualise the above scriptures and discern what Jesus did for us. In other words, this scripture says the Lord's table should be taken in reverence and honouring one another.

Another view of discerning the Lord's body is how we treat each other. The Bible tells us to honour one another (Romans 12:10).

We are one body in Christ (Romans 12:5), and we must treat each other in honour. This is also part of discerning the Lord's body.

The Will of God

We are told not to be unwise but to understand the will of the Lord. It takes discernment to understand the will of God.

"Wherefore be ye not unwise, but understanding what the will of the Lord is" (Ephesians 5:17).

We are also told to prove what is acceptable unto the Lord (Ephesians 5:10).

So, how do we do that?

It will depend on what it is, but the first screen is, "What does God's Word say about this"? If it is obvious in Scripture, we can discern God's will on that matter.

A good example would be, does God want me well? Scripture is clear, and He took our sicknesses and diseases (Matthew 8:17). Therefore, we know God wants us well.

This is just one of many examples that is very clear in Scripture.

However, when we want to decide who to marry, when to go into ministry, or what job to take, it is wisdom to discern God's will and not make our own natural choices. This will then involve praying, seeking the Lord, checking our hearts, asking for wise counsel, etc., depending on the situation and how we are led.

The Value in Others

It is safe to say that lack of discernment is why people unnecessarily abort relationships. We need to discern the value in other people.

We are told to honour one another.

You might not necessarily agree with everything a person does but appreciating and discerning the value in others will ensure that you intentionally keep and cultivate some relationships.

THE IMPORTANCE OF SPIRITUAL DISCERN...

We are told to know no man after the flesh (2 Corinthians 5:16).

This is where investing in the future generation is so important. Hence, if you have an opportunity to invest in the younger generation, consider it. It does not necessarily need to be money; it could just be your time and being there for a person.

Moses' parents discerned their son's value when he was only a few months old. Thank God they did and did not allow Moses to be destroyed.

"By faith Moses, when he was born, was hid three months of his parents, because they saw he was a proper child; and they were not afraid of the king's commandment" (Hebrews 11:23).

We can all read about Moses today because his parents discerned his worth from a young age.

Discerning What the Lord is saying

Has the Lord spoken to you, and you did not discern or understand it? As the ways of the Lord are far above our ways, sometimes it takes time to fully understand what the Lord is saying or has said to us.

In the gospel, we find the phrase, "as they were able to hear" (Mark 4:33). In other words, the Lord spoke what they could hear.

There will always be times when the full implication of what the Lord is saying to us will unfold over time. However, there are things we need to discern fairly immediately.

Sometimes, we would need to ask questions and ask the Holy Spirit to reveal what is being said. Sometimes, we would need to seek godly counsel.

We are not to find ourselves being dull of hearing (Hebrews 5:11).

A good example of different degrees of perception when the Lord speaks can be found in the Book of John:

"Now is my soul troubled; and what shall I say? Father, save me from this hour: but for this cause came I unto this hour. Father, glorify thy name. ***Then came there a voice from heaven, saying, I have both glorified it, and will glorify it again.*** *The people therefore, that stood by, and heard it, said that it thundered: others said, An angel spake to him"* (John 12:27-29).

THE IMPORTANCE OF SPIRITUAL DISCERN...

From the above scripture, we can see what the voice said. However, some that heard it said "it thundered" while others said "an angel spake to Him".

It is obvious some people could not hear it.

Have you ever looked back at your life and said, *"I can now see what the Lord was trying to tell me"*? We need to pray for quick discernment, so we do not lose out unnecessarily.

Times and Seasons

The Bible says that to everything, there is a time and a season for every purpose under heaven (Ecclesiastes 3:1).

Not knowing times and seasons can be costly.

The Bible says that the children of Issachar had understanding of the times and knew what Israel ought to do (1 Chronicles 12:32).

We need to ask the Lord and be led by the Holy Spirit to be able to discern times and seasons.

Chapter 7

Scriptures about Discernment

Now, let us look at a few scriptures that speak about discernment:

"Beloved, believe not every spirit, but try the spirits whether they are of God: because many false prophets are gone out into the world" (1 John 4:1).

The above scripture tells us to try the spirits.

For every one that useth milk is unskilful in the word of righteousness: for he is a babe. But strong meat belongeth to them that are of full age, even those who by reason of use have their senses exercised to discern both good and evil (Hebrews 5:13-14).

THE IMPORTANCE OF SPIRITUAL DISCERN...

From this scripture, we can see that good discernment comes first by growth and then by reason of use.

"For the word of God is living and powerful, and sharper than any two-edged sword, piercing even to the division of soul and spirit, and of joints and marrow, and is a discerner of the thoughts and intents of the heart" (Hebrews 4:12).

Here, we can see that God's word can divide between the soul and spirit. Therefore, we should also allow the word of God to discern the thoughts and intents of our hearts. In other words, between what is acceptable and unacceptable to the Lord.

The remedy is always to repent and make the necessary adjustments in our hearts to align with the truth:

"Judge not according to the appearance, but judge righteous judgment" (John 7:24).

When the Lord sent Samuel to choose a king for Israel that the Lord had already chosen, the Lord told Samuel not to look at outward appearance:

"And it came to pass, when they were come, that he looked on Eliab, and said, Surely the Lord's anointed is before him. But the Lord said unto Samuel, Look not on his coun-

tenance, or on the height of his stature; because I have refused him: for the Lord seeth not as man seeth; for man looketh on the outward appearance, but the Lord looketh on the heart" (1 Samuel 16:6-7).

The only way we will not miss it is to see with the Lord's eyes.

"*But the natural man receiveth not the things of the Spirit of God: for they are foolishness unto him: neither can he know them, because they are spiritually discerned*" (1 Corinthians 2:14).

The things of the Spirit of God are spiritually discerned.

Chapter 8

How to Sharpen Our Discernment

So, how can we increase and sharpen our discernment?

We Need to be Students of the Word of God

The Bible tells us that the Word of Christ should dwell richly in us (Colossians 3:16).

The more familiar we are with the word of God, the easier it will be for us to discern both good and evil, between good doctrine and bad doctrine. Therefore, it is crucial we study and read the Bible ourselves.

Learning to Yield and Walk With the Holy Spirit

We need to learn how to yield and listen to Him. You might just have a check in your spirit or sense that something is not proper.

Having a Vibrant Prayer Life

Having a vibrant prayer life will help us sharpen our discernment. In the place of prayer, we will be able to discern the will of the Father, and the Holy Spirit will bring truth to our remembrance.

Could this be one reason Jesus rose up a great while before dawn to pray (Mark 1:35)? We can see from the life of our Lord Jesus Christ during His earthly ministry that He operated in spiritual discernment.

Always Commit Your Ways Unto the Lord

We must always commit our ways unto the Lord if we want the Lord's perspective on a matter. This will increase our discernment.

Only the Lord knows the end of that matter you are about to say yes to; only the Lord knows the future and heart of a person you are about to commit to.

Scriptures say we should commit all our ways unto the Lord:

"Trust in the Lord with all thine heart; and lean not unto thine own understanding. In all thy ways acknowledge him, and he shall direct thy paths" (Proverbs 3:5-6).

If we lean unto our own understanding, we will cut ourselves short of true spiritual discernment, as we would not engage with He who knows all things.

Admit You Can Have Blind Spots

Blind spots are areas in our lives that we are currently unaware of that can cause hindrances in life and making decisions.

There is a reason the Bible asks us to seek counsel:

"Every purpose is established by counsel: and with good advice make war" (Proverbs 20:18).

A good example of this can be found in the life of Moses. It took his father-in-law to make him realise that what he was doing at the time, sitting and judging people almost all day, would have worn him out. At that time, Moses did not know what his perspective could have cost him. Thank God for his father-in-law.

It is obvious that this must have been a blind spot for Moses, as he had no idea what the implication of his actions could have cost him and the people. In other words, in that particular situation, Moses had no discernment:

"*And it came to pass on the morrow, that Moses sat to judge the people: and the people stood by Moses from the morning unto the evening. And when Moses' father in law saw all that he did to the people, he said, What is this thing that thou doest to the people? why sittest thou thyself alone, and all the people stand by thee from morning unto even? And Moses said unto his father in law, Because the people come unto me to enquire of God: When they have a matter, they come unto me; and I judge between one and another, and I do make them know the statutes of God, and his laws. And Moses' father in law said unto him, The thing that thou doest is not good. **Thou wilt surely wear away, both thou, and this people that is with thee: for this thing is too heavy for thee; thou art not able to perform it thyself alone. Hearken now unto my voice, I will give thee counsel, and God shall be with thee: Be thou for the people to God-ward, that thou mayest bring the causes unto God***" (Exodus 18:13-19).

THE IMPORTANCE OF SPIRITUAL DISCERN...

This is one reason we need to run things by people who are more experienced than us or those we have permitted to speak into our lives.

Chapter 9

Cost of Lack of Discernment

We can all look back and see some wrong decisions we have made due to a lack of spiritual discernment. This is why we need to learn how to walk with the person of the Holy Spirit.

The cost of a lack of spiritual discernment will depend on what the situation is.

It can cost us relationships. For instance, we may not discern why a person is in our lives until they leave. Sometimes, we may push them away years or months down the road before we realise what we have done.

We can miss our time of visitation if we lack discernment. This is what happened to Jerusalem during

THE IMPORTANCE OF SPIRITUAL DISCERN...

the earthly ministry of our Lord Jesus Christ (Luke 13:34).

We can get involved with the wrong people, make costly wrong decisions that could be costly, the list goes on.

Chapter 10

Good News

The good news is that we have what it takes to walk in spiritual discernment. The Greater One who knows all things lives in us (1 John 4:4), and He shows us things to come (John 16:13).

We just have to acknowledge the great helper the Lord has sent to help us in this life (John 14:18).

The Lord wants the best for us and loves us (1 John 4:7).

Jesus Christ has come to give us life and life more abundantly (John 10:10).

Therefore, God is on our side, and the Lord has given us what we require that pertains to life (2 Peter 1:3).

THE IMPORTANCE OF SPIRITUAL DISCERN...

We may make mistakes, but we will learn from them. We must remember that we live in a fallen world.

Chapter 11

Conclusion

We have seen the importance of spiritual discernment, and we need to start walking in discernment because we live in a fallen world.

Partnering with the Holy Spirit and training our spiritual senses will save us from many bumps along life's journey.

Making hasty decisions and rushing into relationships that turn out bitter will be put to an end.

Let us admit we need help and engage with the person of the Holy Spirit.

In this life, we cannot just always rely on our physical perceptions, as there are many other factors that will require spiritual discernment to identify.

Salvation Prayer

Father God, I come to you in Jesus' name. I admit that I am a sinner, and I now receive the sacrifice that Jesus Christ paid for me.

I confess with my mouth the Lord Jesus, and I believe in my heart that God raised Him from the dead.

I now declare that Jesus Christ is my Lord and Saviour.

Thank you, Father, for saving me in Jesus' name.

I am now your child. Amen.

If you've said this prayer for the first time, send an email to bisiwriter@outlook.com. Start reading your Bible and ask the Lord to guide you to a good church.

About The Author

Bisi Oladipupo has been a Christian for many years and lives in the United Kingdom with her family.

Bisi attended a few Bible colleges, and she has completed a diploma in Biblical Studies from a UK Bible college.

She is a teacher of God's Word, coordinates Bible studies, and has a YouTube channel at https://www.youtube.com/c/BisiOladipupo123.

Her author page is www.bisiwriter.com

She writes regularly, and her blog website is www.inspiredwords.org

You can contact Bisi by email at bisiwriter@outlook.com.

Also By Bisi

The Twelve Apostles of Jesus Christ: Lessons We Can Learn

The Lord's Cup in Communion: The Significance of taking the Lord's Supper

Different Ways to Receive Healing from Scripture and Walk in Health

Believing on The Name of Jesus Christ: What Every Believer Needs to Know

The Mind and Your Christian Walk: The Impact of the mind on our Christian walk

Relationship Skills in the Bible: Scriptural Principles of relating to others

The Nature of God's Kingdom: The Characteristics of the Kingdom of God

The Person of the Holy Spirit

BISI OLADIPUPO

41 Insights from the Book of Revelation

www.ingramcontent.com/pod-product-compliance
Lightning Source LLC
Chambersburg PA
CBHW030045100526
44590CB00011B/337